Midas

Living with a Bird in the Hood

DONITA KORDONOWY

PAGE PUBLISHING
Conneaut Lake, PA

First originally published by Page Publishing 2022

ISBN 978-1-6624-8298-4 (pbk)
ISBN 978-1-6624-8299-1 (digital)

Printed in the United States of America

To those I love: my daughter, son, and my critters—every one of them (past, present, and any that I get in the future).

Introduction

When you love animals, you help when and where possible. I love each and every one of my animals, pups, cats, and birds, even Midas the Second.

Midas has added laughter, stopped arguments, and will amuse everyone that has either met or read some of our conversations. Midas's Laugh Corner was started on Facebook to share his brilliant wit (said with rolling eyes) and sarcastic remarks with friends and family.

I hope you enjoy his story, which is told using his actual words and is NOT EDITED for children, as Midas does swear.

Animals in My House

Cats are Shadow, Spitfire, and Magick. Birds are Midas and Onyx (lovebird). Dogs—some that Midas name have passed; others are almost as big of pain as Midas. Cleopatra, Anthony, and Isabella are my thirteen-year-old (almost fourteen) pups.

Sometimes, the journey needs to be made, the heart needs to break, and the tears fall in order to see the road that we are supposed to be on. Sometimes you need to be lost before you know where you are supposed to be.

Donita Kordonowy

Chapter 1

April is always an interesting month for me because it's when I first realize that winter blues are actually on their way out to make way for spring cleaning, taxes, my birthday, and, the best part, summer. In its anticipation of summer, April is a month of new growth; trees are budding, flowers, which lay dormant all winter, are peeking through the warm ground, birds are building nests in hopes of starting their families, the grass is turning green, the sun is out a wee bit longer, and the air feels a wee bit warmer. Spring is the second-best season of the year and prepares you for the best season, summer.

April 2007 was almost like all the other Aprils I have experienced, with the exception of that is also when Midas the Second, an African gray parrot, moved into our home. His personal story prior to moving to Rochester, New York, is short. Nobody, and by nobody, I mean no human being I know or don't know, had any information about him. They did not know what he ate (favorite food always helps when working with a new critter) or his favorite toys or if he even had any. But worse than anything else, they did not even know what his name was.

We already know that Midas wasn't born but hatched somewhere between the time the world was created and prior to the time that his first owner could no longer care for him, which was in April 2007. Roughly we figured he was an old man of about twenty-five to forty years of age because he came with ruff-looking feathers, and he really had to look at his food to see what it was. Of course, he could possibly be checking his food to make sure he wasn't being poisoned.

Let's back up a bit and give a wee bit more information on how he came to live with us or as much of it as we could find out. I will also include a wee bit of information about my background with parrots.

First, let's start with my history, and since I am a boring person, there is not much to tell. I have over twenty-five years of bird, aka parrot, knowledge. I spent a number of years rescuing parrots, determined after working with them, for a few weeks or sometimes months, what would be best for the parrot. I would put the parrots into one of three categories, which consists of petables, watchers, and unpredictables.

The first and best of the categories is the petables. Petables are the parrots that, after working with them, could once more enter a family as a true pet. This means that the parrot knows the commands, and with a little work (sometimes a lot of work and a few blood donations), they will execute simple commands, such as step up without taking a bite out of your hand. They also know when you say "no bite," they will loosen the grip of their beak. With more work, they would learn more commands or even more complex commands, depending on the family and the amount of training they provide. But the family would be instructed that they would need to handle the parrot daily, along with going through all the commands with the parrot, or the parrot will slide backward.

The second category is watchers. The watchers don't want to be handled but enjoy being around people and interacting with them on a limited basis. Midas the Second falls into this category. Midas does know how to step up, but he bites and will draw blood each time. Watchers love being part of the family but don't want or are unable to retain that safe pet category. I can work Midas's cage, but Angel, my daughter, cannot. He attacks her every time she tries to get food, dishes, or clean his cage.

Watchers normally will not talk when people are in the same room, but they know everything (or so it seems) that happens in the household (or, in our case, the whole darn neighborhood). This is why I call them watchers. They seem to keep track of everyone, including the fur babies (cats and/or dogs). If you are experienced with parrots and their habits, you can leave them out of their cage to play in a bird playpen, but I would keep wings, nails, and beaks trimmed just in case. You would also want a safe way to get them back in their cage. Midas the Second will step up on a broom handle, and that is how he gets back in his cage when he escapes. Midas loves "broom rides," which allows him to pretend he is flying.

Just so that you are aware, if Midas gets out of his cage while we are not home, he is safe from all animals in the house because they are kenneled while I am not home to keep them all safe.

The worse of categories and most unpredictable are those I do call the unpredictables (don't you think this would make a great television series). Neither yours nor their safety is guaranteed when handled, even the most experienced will be bit, or the parrot will get hurt. They would rather rip you apart than be around you and seem to only squawk at the top of their voice. They don't like anyone, including sometimes other parrots. If possible, I would see if there was another parrot that they would bond with and let them live the life of the breeder parrot if they choose and is young enough, or you let them spend the rest of their life in a nice area off-limits to people and other birds.

It is difficult to work their cages because they attack when you get too close. Sometimes, with a mate, they calm down a wee bit, but they are still unpredictable and not nice. If you were lucky and they chose a mate they liked, you would end up with babies if the bird is not too old. If they didn't like any of the possible mates, it could be a gory scene you come upon the next day with no survivors. They are the hardest to deal with because there is no given outcome, and they are unpredictable in their behavior.

For some reason, I am not sure why, but some parrots are so frustrated and mad, probably with the person who abused and/or neglected them, that they believe everyone and every-thing in the world is that way. Parrots, like ele-phants, do not forget. If they were abused by a man who slapped them with their baseball hat each time they walked in the room, they will attack all men wearing baseball hats. It's the hat that is the threat, and they concen-trate on ending that hat's life and whomever it is attached to. Hopefully, in time with gen-tle words and proper nutrition, the parrot will come around and be tested again. I test periodically in hopes of improvement, but most of the time, there is no change. Lucky for me, not many parrots that I rescued fell into the unpredictable category, thank goodness.

I can also tell you everyone you meet who works with parrots feels they are the "go-to guru" who knows the best way to take care of that bird you just got. They are the expert on food, cages, and what is best for the parrot and you. If you go through a pet store, they will try to sell you the most expensive items on the shelf for your new bird and just give you a little information on the bird itself. If you are new to birds, listen to everyone, but do not believe that what they say is the absolute truth because, like kids, there will be that one bird you can never fit in any mold, and I had a few of those.

There are a few dos and don'ts, which are common sense with animals in general, such as parrots need a variety of fruits and vegetables. Seeds and nuts are like giving your human child a handful of candy for their supper. It is the same with parrots; they will enjoy them as a training treat but don't use seeds or nuts as their main meal. Parrots cannot digest the toxins in chocolate or avocadoes. So even though we would love to share everything with our feathered friends, we need to do so wisely, avoiding foods and drinks that will harm our beloved feathered friend.

Due to rescuing many birds from budgies on up, I decided to open my own bird store. The ones which made great pets I took down to see if I could adopt them into loving homes. I added consignment birds for those who wanted to sell their birds and bird-sitting, which allowed me to handle and learn to respect many types of parrots and parakeets (and fall in love with many more species). I have many bird stories, but most here will pertain to Midas the Second.

Sadly, my store was short-lived due to divorce. I found that those who brought their parrots to the store to sell didn't want them back when I called to have them come get them. And yes, I truly miss the happy noise of all the parrots, and I would not trade that for the world. When I moved to Rochester, New York, I came with my two kids, three dogs, and fifty birds from budgies to African gray (Midas the First). Shortly after moving into my house, and in the middle of the night on a day, which turned out to be the coldest day of that winter, my furnace went out. I lost my parrots due to the cold that invaded our tropical-sounding paradise. Casualties included my beloved Midas the First. It was one of the saddest days of my life and one I never want to repeat.

Enough about me because I am that boring person who rattles on about all animals. I am here to let you know that Midas the Second is funny, outgoing, and very loud if he chooses to be. If you are in a bad mood, your mood will be lifted, if not for just a little while, when arguing with Midas. Even though he keeps us entertained, many do not believe that the conversations are true unless they experience them for themselves. This is difficult because he doesn't say much when you try to record him and seldom speaks when you are in the room with him. Just like a child, he speaks when you want silence and is silent when you want him to talk.

Storm

June 2, 2018

Midas's Laugh Corner

Dogs are barking.

Midas yells: You bark like a girl.

Chapter 2

A close family friend who thinks of me as her mom called my daughter, Angel, about a parrot who was going to be turned loose outside if no one claimed him before the end of the day. She wanted to know if we would be interested since I lost my African gray five years prior. Because of working with parrots prior, Angel didn't hesitate to tell Sisi to get him. Sisi even drove him from the Poughkeepsie, New York area all the way to Rochester, New York, so that she and Angel could surprise me for my birthday with an African gray parrot. I won't tell them that I heard most of the conversation, at least on Angel's side. Sadly, Sisi could not find out any information about him as his human was being put into a nursing home due to dementia. Because of this, no one knew his name, favorite food, or toys—no information, including if he could talk.

Now let me insert here a wee bit of parrot information for those who never had a bird for a pet. Some birds, regardless of the type of parrot, never learn to talk or choose not to talk for whatever reason. If you start with whistles, since this is the easiest to learn for parrots, they may only choose to whistle and never learn beyond whistling to communicate with people. If they do talk, when in a new location, they become shy and will not talk, and one may not know until they choose to open up and start talking once more, but you need to know that may never happen. Just like people, trauma of losing a beloved human affects everyone differently, and that would also include their ability to vocalize.

Even now, Midas seldom talks when we are in the same room or new people are around. He will wait more often than not until you are in another room to talk to you. Also, depending on the parrot, the voice they use can sound like people you know to barely audible whispers. Budgies (better known as a parakeet) are noted whisperers, and Quaker parakeets have a garbled voice, sounding like they are talking with a mouth full of food or marbles. African gray parrots, on the other hand, can sound like anyone in your household: your son, daughter, significant other, and even the dreaded mother-in-law if she visits often enough. They can also sound like any animal you have, other birds (including the outside birds), cats, dogs, or any barnyard animal you may have. This makes it difficult to tell who is talking to you unless you are truly paying attention to who is home when you are asked about something from another room or when they are replying to your questions from an unseen location.

Midas is not the first bird we worked with where we didn't know the past or were given misinformation. Sometimes it is not the past but the future that is important. We did it once, we could do it again, and because we had faith, I named him Midas the Second, partly because I was still missing the first Midas and partly because I felt Midas is a fitting name for an African gray parrot.

Looking at Midas, you could tell he was an older bird as his feathers were beaten and ragged; he spent most of his time at the bottom of his cage, looking defeated. He would look really close at his food, making me think his eyesight was diminished. Thinking back now, maybe he was trying to figure out what I was feeding him, especially if it was something he never had. Today, now that I know Midas's temperament and habits, he may have thought we were trying to poison him, and he was checking to see if he could spot anything that could be lethal on his food.

Exactly how old Midas is would be anyone's guess, but because it was stated that the woman who had him, had him for a very long time. How long is a "long time?" Because of what we observed and how Midas stayed more at the bottom of his cage, which he still does today, we put him in the "old" category. Because of his actions and his ragged look, it wasn't uncommon for us to make the statement, "I don't believe he is going to live very long, if he makes it through the heat of summer, I will be surprised." And then it would be, "If he makes it through the cold of winter, I will be surprised." He has surprised us now for almost fifteen years because even though he looks like he is in rough shape, he is still hanging in there with his "sass but no class" attitude. We stopped saying, "I'd be surprised if he makes it through..." because he has continued to surprise us with his determination to be with us. Although recently, those thoughts have been creeping back into my thoughts.

Birds normally molt twice a year, and spring is one of those times. When they molt, their feathers look tattered and rough until they are preened. His feathers are ruffled and ragged, but it is April, and he could be molting, which means new feathers would be coming in, and the old worn feathers falling out, which means once he is done molting, he will have feathers everywhere!

He could also be ragged-looking due to a poor diet. People suffering from dementia and living alone tend to forget to feed themselves right along with their companion pets, which they may have. For whatever the reason, Midas was the only critter they didn't have someone step up to claim, and we are not sure why. It may be because being a larger bird, about twelve inches tall, combined with not being handled in many days, possibly years, was not very friendly.

As I said earlier, I have about twenty-five years of experience working with parrots. Rehabbing a parrot is not for the faint of heart because you are looking at approximately six hundred pounds of pressure per inch of beak. Small birds such as budgie (called parakeets by most people) feel like a hard pinch, hurt for a few, and then it's forgotten. Cockatiels hurt a wee bit more because they have more of a sawing-type bite, a little back and forth of the beak when they bite. Smaller parrots may or may not break skin, but the odds go up with the size of the parrot. An African gray has enough pressure in their beak to break an arm if they want. At the very least, you will have a very nasty and bleeding gash where you were bit, requiring a trip to the emergency room for stitches. They also have nice claws, which are better to cling to keep you from fleeing their grasp while they rip flesh from your bones to appease their evil desire to take over the world.

You also need to know that the wrong move may seriously injure or kill the parrot, so caution is best when working with an unfamiliar parrot or parakeet of any size. You also should be willing to give a little blood if you are determined to handle the bird.

Midas was not willing to take direction of any sort. I could not trust him not to bite at any time, so his cage is located where he is able to keep track of everyone and everything. I knew he would never be a true pet like his namesake, but he does enjoy letting everyone know how he feels. He gets to participate in conversations of his choice and hears everything that goes on in the house and outside in the neighborhood.

Because I work Monday through Friday, I do not know what happens during the day because I am not there. When I get home, I do get some idea of what may have transpired while I was gone. Like the teenage boys yelling at the teenage girls that they are fat (or maybe they may mean "phat," pretty hot and tempting). Or a "hot chick" got out of a car, and the guys are sending catcalls. What happens while I am gone during the day comes out in little bits over time.

Like my daughter coming home after doing laundry, and Midas yells at her, "Hey, Toots, who's your daddy?"

Of course, good manners force her to respond, yelling back, "It's not you!"

When Midas talks, you can't help but respond. I am hoping that we still have many years with Midas, but one never knows with a parrot how long they will live. Parrots, like many animals, hide when they are sick because in the wild, it is survival of the fittest, and so you fake it until it's gone or you are.

Storm

December 15, 2017

Midas's Laugh Corner

Me yelling at a pup to leave the cats alone...

Midas: GET YOUR HANDS OFF ME!

Me and Angel ~~shakes our head~~

Midas: GET YOUR HANDS UP!

WTF has been going on while I have been at work?

Storm

February 4, 2018

Midas's Laugh Corner

Midas: Call me Big Daddy.
Me: Nothing big about Midas.

Chapter 3

In 2002, my kids and I bought a house that was built in 1900 in a nice Italian neighborhood. How could I tell it was an Italian neighborhood, you ask, by the smells flowing through the neighborhood of dinners simmering on the stove in the late afternoon. We loved sitting out on the porch, enjoying the mix of herbs from the various sauces I imagined that was simmering on the stove, waiting for everyone to gather around for a pasta dinner of some sort. I enjoyed it. We would even enjoy our meals and idle conversations on the front porch during the nice weather.

By 2006, the neighborhood was declining rapidly as I found that many of my neighbors were elderly and either moved to a smaller house as they no longer had kids at home, were placed in nursing homes, or passed away. Their cherished home was sold to someone who used it as a rental, or it remained empty for several years and only visited, a.k.a. broken into by kids looking for a place to get out of inclement weather while they partied with friends while avoiding the supervision of parents. Slowly I watched as drug dealers moved in. I felt sorry for my one neighbor. How can you tell someone that their grandsons are selling drugs from Grandma's back porch while she is at the hospital with her ailing husband? After Grandpa passed, they didn't care what Grandma or their mom said; they sold from the front porch along with another handful of front porch salesmen.

The excitement on the block came from the multiple arrests, especially during the summer. There were three or four houses on the block where police were there two or three times a week for either domestic violence or drug raids. It is what happens when houses become rentals with no landlord nearby to complain to about his tenants. As a family, we did well at ignoring what happened in the neighborhood; we watched but did not say a word to anyone. If one is honest, it is a whole lot safer when one ignores the illegal failings of neighbors. And by keeping silent, for the most part, we were left alone.

In the beginning, I went door-to-door asking if the neighbors would stand with me to get the drug dealers out of the neighborhood, but I was told either "why should I worry about them, I have no kids" or "my kids are babies, I don't need to worry about them." One person may want to, but one person alone would be very dangerous, so I dropped it and watched but kept my mouth shut. By this time, we stopped sitting on the front porch as we found what looked like a few bullet holes in the front porch. Too many drug dealers and those who were looking for their services that if we spent any time outside, it was only in the backyard and just long enough for my dogs to do their business and get a little fresh air; nice having small dogs.

And now, Midas is a welcome addition to our household for as long as he wants to be on this earth. From April until mid-October or early November of 2007, Midas didn't say a word. He still looked rough and spent more time at the bottom of his cage with us, stating, "Don't think he will survive much longer" or "I don't believe he will make it through this winter," but he made did. I think he did so just to prove us wrong, which I don't mind being wrong over whether or not it was his time to make it to the rainbow bridge.

Do I absolutely know if Midas is a male or female? No, I don't. But when I first started working with parrots, especially African grays, a breeder stated that 99 percent of the time, a rounded head on an African gray is a male. If the head appears to be flat on an African gray, you have a 99 percent chance that that parrot is going to be a female. Midas the Second has a rounded head, as did Midas the first, who I did have tested to find out his sex, which came back as male. Also, most female birds, whether they have a partner or not, will lay eggs during their adulthood. Of course, with no mate, the eggs are not fertilized and will not hatch. Midas has never laid an egg in the time that he has been with us, which also makes me about 99 percent sure Midas is a male.

Not hearing Midas didn't bother me. Yes, I did wonder if he would or could talk, but if he couldn't, I wasn't concerned because I never knew if he did prior to living with us. For my animals, including Midas, so he would not feel alone, I leave the radio playing to a country station while I am working, and it remains on until bedtime. He gets his dose of country music as I know the verbiage will not be vulgar or upset anyone if he repeats any of it in front of kids.

Then that fatal day came, the one I was waiting for since his arrival, the first time Midas uttered any words in my house that broke his silence forever. He still comes up with words and phrases that shock and leave me wondering, "What the...," because I don't know exactly where he heard everything that he is reciting, but I do know that it is not from the radio.

It was one of those long workdays where it seemed everyone wanted something from you, and it took forever to accomplish while they told you how slow you took because you couldn't get it done fast enough for them. You felt drained and wondered why you are doing this when what you do is not appreciated. Now that work is done, you still must get home and cook, and you are hoping that maybe, with any luck, the kids decided to fix something, anything, so you wouldn't have to. It's cold outside because it is just that time of the year, and light snow is falling, making you drive a wee bit slower, or at least I do.

The wind is blowing the snow in swirls on the road, and all you want is to be home to avoid all the crazy people, drivers, and pedestrians, who don't want to cross the road in a crosswalk to ensure their safety. It seemed longer than normal just to reach the safety and warmth of home. In anticipation of comfy clothes and supper makes you want to get there a wee bit faster, so everything is done sooner.

I walked into the house, took off my coat, and hung it over the stair railing as always. I yell up the stairs to the kids, "I'm home," when a voice from the entryway to the kitchen yells back in a little old lady's voice, "I thought you were in prison." Midas finally broke his silence, making his first words forever imprinted in our memories, and the disbelief and amused smiles etched into our shocked faces when we think about his arrival into our little world.

Okay, I will admit that my jaw dropped, and had to be picked up from the ground. Angel came downstairs, looked at me, and said something to the fact, "Was that Midas?"

I replied, "Yes, it was Midas."

I would state, for the record, that sometimes work does feel like prison (but I wouldn't admit that to the warden, I mean my boss). Because of what Midas said, we wonder to this day who the previous owner of this bird was, or, at the very least, who did the owner associated with to be thinking that someone was in prison when they came to visit. Lots of questions with no answers coming from Midas.

For some of the phrases, we had to do a little research to see if we could find the meaning. They would have either been used by ex-cons who either dealt drugs or were friends of drug dealers or users.

Being November and living in snow country, we would keep track of the weather, and I would periodically ask the kids what the weather was doing.

One night, after asking, Angel stated that it was starting to snow, to which Midas replied, "Just put the snow down."

Okay, nice to know that you can, but after researching the phrase, we don't believe he was referring to the weather giving the impression if Granny wasn't a jailbird, had jailbirds for family members; she, at the very least, had friends who did time.

Lucky for us, Midas moved on to other phrases just as entertaining as the snow comments, regardless of what he was actually referring to, fell to the wayside as just temporary amusement for us and Midas. Midas does pay attention to what happens outside and inside the house and never fails to amuse us with witty comments as if he knows exactly what we are talking about.

Storm

August 20, 2012

Midas's Laugh for the Day:

Storm...Keep moving, Anthony (my pup)...outside.

    Midas..."Are you walking?"

    Storm..."Yes, I'm walking."

    Midas..."Did it Hurt?"

    Angel Roze bursts out laughing...at this time...For Sale...One Smart Mouthed Parrot...gotta love him.

Angel Is with Storm

November 12, 2017

Midas just yelled, "Bring me a puppy!"
　　Uh...no!

Chapter 4

There are many short one-liner remarks that come out of Midas, like calling me "the warden" yesterday when I was giving him his breakfast. Yes, I respond when he comments, and sometimes his answer surprises me even more.

In the beginning, Midas was constantly yelling at Joey or Maddy (could be Matty) and occasionally Cassandra for various misdoings. I know I was hoping that Joey and Maddy were safe and doing well because it seemed like they were always in trouble for little things. The funny part is that when Midas would yell at them, he would use a little old lady's voice, so you would wonder if it was Grandma yelling at grandchildren or kids who provoked their mother while visiting Grandma or neighborhood kids terrorizing the little old lady next door.

When the phone rang, usually one of my kids would answer because it was usually one of their friends calling. Digaaz, my son, usually was gaming at night, which meant that his friends would call to see when he was on, and if he was playing, where he was in the game, or they would discuss life in general. My daughter would have either work, calling her in early or friends calling, just to chitchat and catch up on each other's life.

Now when the phone rings, Midas would yell, "Answer the damn phone, I'm on the pot!"

Yes, at that time, Midas was still using the little old lady's voice, causing Angel and I to look at each other and just shake our heads and laugh.

Midas also started yelling, "Is it ready yet?" when you are cooking or making popcorn.

Yes, when he yells, you react by "yelling" back, "No, it's not ready yet!"

For the next twenty minutes, you are going back and forth between the two of you on whether the popcorn or supper is ready or not. It's like the irritating kid asking, "Are we there yet?" every two or three minutes.

Yes, Midas receives popcorn before the salt and butter are added, and depending on what's for supper, he may get some of it also. While Midas indulges in his recently acquired food, we indulge in the peace and quiet.

The yelling to ask if it is ready yet also happens in the morning when you are preparing breakfast for the animals. Yes, my critters get breakfast. My dogs get half of a hard-boiled egg along with kibble every morning. It is alternated with green peppers and carrots or other vegetables (three days a week), and on Tuesdays and Thursdays, with their kibble, they will get a changing variety of apple slices, dehydrated food, broccoli, and or cucumber slices, and bone broth. Midas and Onyx (a lovebird) would get bird pellets, along with an assortment of fruits, vegetables, and nuts every day.

While fixing everything, Midas keeps you company complaining about various things such as "is it ready yet?"

Of course, if you don't get his breakfast to him fast enough, when you put the dish in his cage, he will grab it and slam the door closed, so he can eat. He starts with his favorites, throwing to the bottom of his cage the parts of food he wants to eat later or does not like. I do like to offer him different things in hopes that he will indulge. Sometimes, he does eat them; the next time, he tosses them, hence, no consistency with his food choices.

Every once in a while, he still yells at Cassandra, Matty/Maddy, and Joey, but not as often as he did in his early days. If nothing else, Cassandra, Matty/Maddy, and Joey, if you know who you are, Midas (not sure of what his real name was) still thinks of you.

Angel Was with Storm

January 14, 2017

Midas's Laugh Corner

Storm and I were in the kitchen while she was cooking supper, and well...Midas...need I say anything more.

Midas yells: I'm on my period! (I
  might point out we never say
  that; we have other phrases
  we use.)
Angel: You want some chocolate?
Midas: I'll kick your ass!

   Storm and I were both laughing, of course, and he's mumbling under his breath, and then on the way upstairs, he whines.

Midas: I'm faaaaaaaaaaaaaat.
~shakes head~ Really, Midas?

Storm

October 21, 2017

Midas words of wisdom:

You're the Mom, and you just don't care.

Chapter 5

A couple that my daughter knew was having trouble not only financially but were living in a depressed state where jobs were hard to find asked us for help. Now that I know more, not sure how many were lies on her part. To top it off, his brother was kicking them to the curb (as did I, but I didn't wait for over two years).

The agreement was we would help them get back on their feet, and they would acquire work; pay us rent until they found their own place within two months, three months at the very latest. I told both Angel and Patty that in the end, they may no longer be friends. Patty stated nothing would ruin their friendship. I always believed you could either be friends or roommates, never both, and in this case, I was right.

When Patty and John arrived, we gave them our schedule, stating that they don't mess with my animals as they are on our schedule. Patty didn't appreciate that because she loved cats, and my then ten-month-old kittens were in training and were on my schedule. I was only expecting them to be here maximum of two months.

Needless to say, Midas heard more than even I would like because Patty was full of cow patties. She wanted to be catered, to which her husband was willing to do, but I was not. They never paid rent, bought groceries, or even offered to help with normal living chores, such as dishes or cooking.

Patty was a thirty-plus-year veteran of diabetes. Every diabetic I know knew exactly when they needed insulin and when they needed a little more sugar. I cannot prove otherwise, but I believe Patty used this to get her husband to cater to her wishes, including calling off work or canceling interviews.

Every time John had an interview between three and four o'clock in the morning (workdays sucked because of this), she would have what I called a diabetic episode when her sugar level dropped to dangerous levels close to diabetic coma or death.

John told us that he always stayed home and helped her recover as it took her some time to "get back to normal." He has lost jobs due to too many missed days from his work helping his wife. If he missed an interview, there was no phone call to cancel and reschedule; it was blown off like no big deal.

I am not saying that taking care of a spouse or a loved one is wrong, but you have to make decisions, have priorities, and stop making excuses for their continued emergencies, and either has a back-up plan so you can still work or be honest that there is more going on than you can handle.

Patty did nothing all day. We would get home from work and would have to cook supper, not just for us but for two additional people, in which one was home all day. Patty left a trail of coffee from the kitchen to the bedroom, which is how I knew she left the bed. She was in bed when we left for work, still in pajamas, and in bed when we got home from work. At times, she would be rude, using her diabetes as an excuse not to do anything. When it didn't fly with me, she not only disrespected me but Angel. That was when their friendship went downhill.

Yes, I admit it; I lost it. I would start telling her to put her "big girl panties on" and be a big girl. She needed to stop using her diabetes as a way of controlling her husband, which he said she wasn't, but I told him when he caves in and stays home to "keep her company" while stabilizing her diabetes; he is. When he didn't go to a job interview or work, he was doing exactly what she wanted. I also told him to take a look at all the times when she had episodes and what he had planned for the day, and doing so, opened his eyes—very wide. John asked what he should do, and me being tired of her cow patty ways, I told him that from now on, she should go to the emergency room, and he continued to work or job interview. He needed to do what was best for him and his family. Doctors and nurses are much more qualified to stabilize her sugar levels than he, and he needed to get on his feet financially.

It's now going on about four months of paying all their living expenses when we found out that my kids' half-brother was coming in hopes of new beginnings. Patty and John were to be gone by end of April, first part of May at the latest but knew we were expecting Cass and his wife in July. John is the only one working with a very part-time job and no apartment or full-time job in sight for either John or Patty. And this is where it started going downhill even more.

I lost all patience with Patty, and at four in the morning, after who knows how many times, she disrupted my sleep, so I told her husband to take her to the emergency so he could work that day. That night, when I got home from work, I informed them; they had two weeks to get their crap together because, regardless, they will be gone.

Cass and his wife were nowhere, sharing bedroom space with John and Patty because it was the only room I could put them. Yes, I could have shared a room with Angel, but in my house, I am not moving out of my room to accommodate someone who didn't appreciate the help they were receiving.

This is where Patty had enough and moved into a homeless shelter and later moved back to the west coast to be nearer to her family. She was upset with John because when she gave him the choice of going with her or staying where he was, he chose to stay and listen to me and concentrate on getting a full-time job. Sadly (and totally not my intention), they parted ways.

They both, after some months, ended up going home to their parents (one west coast and the other southwestern part of the state). I wish them both the best, but the stealing of what little money I was saving for Christmas was the final straw. Do I know who stole? Nope, but I do have three possibilities, and by end of September, everyone was gone. To this day, neither have thanked me nor my daughter for helping nor have they paid anything during the seven months they were here.

Now, after all this time, this is where Midas once more starts to vocalize. It took Patty leaving before he once more really found his voice. I am not saying he was silent; he just wasn't as vocal as he normally was.

John comes downstairs, getting ready to leave for his part-time job. Midas is doing his normal off sounds like the microwave going off or bells or whistles, and then asks John if he has on his "granny panties." John about lost it but took it all in stride. Yes, for the most part of their stay, Midas was mostly silent, which does not mean he did not talk; it means he didn't talk like he normally did and nothing like when it is just me and my kids in the house.

Once Patty left, Midas became more vocal. My guess is, Midas doesn't want anyone competing for attention, and if there is a drama queen around, he listens to use against us later. It took a while before he stopped asking if you put on your big girl panties.

Storm

October 7, 2018

I close the house for the night, saying good night and I love you to
my critter-babies...tonight; Midas
replied with, "It's your job."

Chapter 6

As I stated in the title of this book, I live in the hood, and part of living in an unsavory part of town is you have no control over what your "neighbors" do during the day or night. You also don't know what a parrot with the intelligence of a five- or six-year-old kid will hear and repeat.

It just so happened to be a summer night at about two thirty in the morning when everyone should be in bed sleeping. I know we were until the neighbors decided it was a good time to wake up the whole f——ing street with their fighting. And yes, I do swear.

We shouldn't be surprised when there was fighting on the street because there normally were police at one of several houses on the block a few times a week for domestic disturbances, especially during the summer. Guess when the temperature rises, so do the tempers.

We were awoken because of people fighting right outside of our house (this is where I usually ask, "Why me, Lord?" because it was a work night). No surprise to the fighting, but a little surprised because this time, it was two women in the middle of the street that were fighting over some dude they both were dating (using the term loosely). And the guy was trying to get them to quiet down or each go home. Thought just crossed my mind that both must have arrived about the same time at his house for a late-night dancing between the sheets; otherwise, how else could they meet— that part we will leave to others to figure out.

Both women started name-calling, each yelling at the top of their voice for the whole block to hear, truly giving the definition of a *lady* a whole new meaning. They were cussing each other out and basically having little shoving matches with each other, daring the other to take it to the next level so that one or the other could show the other woman how much of a thug, for lack of a better word, that they were.

One gal apparently took it to the next level, physically ripping off the wig of the other gal, and with the wig in her hand, started running toward the top of the street (it is a one-way street). I am not sure if she lived on the street or was visiting, or maybe it was where her car was parked if she was over visiting her male friend.

The gal who lost her wig started running after her, screaming, "My hair! My hair! Gimmie my hair back!"

We didn't think much about it until a few days later when Angel and I were having a disagreement over who remembers now what it was, but it must have triggered in Midas about the gals fighting a few nights before.

In the middle of our argument, Midas yells, "Gimmie my hair, I want my hair back!" It relieved the tension between Angel and me, and we both burst out laughing, and in unison, yelling back at Midas, "You don't have any hair!"

We never found out which two gals were fighting over the one guy, but we still hear about Midas wanting his hair from time to time in which we remind him that he doesn't have any hair.

Storm Is with Angel

October 21, 2021

Those who are up on the slangs… Midas yelled, "Hey, Tootsie Roll, come here!" Can you explain to us what he means…lmao.

Chapter 7

Now that we know Midas better, one disclaimer that Angel and I always make and one that my daughter especially makes when she does live videos is "not responsible for what comes out of Midas's mouth or what you believe you heard him say." Sadly, if you want him to talk, he is silent, and if you want him to be silent, you can't shut him up.

The city didn't like how I did my outside stairs. Okay, to be honest, my son was the one building the stairs for me, and I was telling him how I wanted them done. When the city checked them out, they didn't like my choice of stairs as per city inspector, "they were not up to the city's code." Because my son didn't have the time at that time to redo his work per the city's expectations due to his work schedule, vehicle issues, and weather not cooperating, my daughter decided to hire a friend and her significant other who does handiwork. For the record, I no longer like my outside stairs, but they are up to city code, but that is another matter altogether. And I have to admit they do look pretty good even if I don't like them.

Due to the use of power tools to cut the wood to length for the stairs being built, extension cords had to be run outside, which was plugged into the electrical sockets in the foyer of the house. Because of this, I knew Midas could hear us talking and, in time, would say something, so I told Phil that any verbiage or screams that he heard or believes he heard coming out of the house would be from Midas, and I am not responsible.

With a puzzled look on his face, he politely asked me what I meant by this. I explained to Phil that I have an African gray who is not always polite and will give his opinion from time to time whether it is wanted or not and sometimes doesn't use appropriate language "for company."

Phil said, "No problem, it's okay," probably thinking that I was just being weird or getting senile. Let's just say Midas did not disappoint, and Phil's face was one of shock and disbelief.

Angel and I were talking with Phil while he was working, asking questions like how I would like this or that and how many stairs I would like to come down from the porch. It was just a general conversation regarding the work he was going to be doing and some of the regulations that the city wanted him to use when he built the stairs. He also reminded us, since we were outside, that we would not be able to go into the house through the front door while he was working as it was a big step up at the time and a safety hazard.

After about a half-hour of work and various discussions of everything that was going on in the world since it is 2020 and COVID-19 was just letting up somewhat, people were in hopes of returning to a near-normal life. Phil asked a question, which we no longer remember, but before we could answer, he got a response from Midas, which was a very loud, "Fuck, yeah."

With a look of bewilderment still on his face, Phil asks, "Did he just say, 'Fuck, yeah'?" Angel and I burst out laughing, looked at each other and then Phil, and said, most likely as we were out of hearing range but know Midas is not a saint.

Phil then called his girlfriend and asked Beth if she knew about Midas. When she said yes, he then asked why she didn't ever mention him. She was probably used to us posting his comments here and there on social media, mainly Facebook, and never gave it a second, thought although he may not have realized it was us she was referring to when she mentioned the parrot.

Because he didn't want to miss the next "fuck yeah," I believe it took Phil a wee bit longer than it would have normally taken him to do the work. The little bit of time that he interacted with Midas, Phil enjoyed it. Some days it is difficult to work because you are waiting on a bird to respond. Best part was that Phil stated that he felt like Midas was actually responding to the questions appropriately (including using swear words).

A few months later, Phil and Beth came over to clean up a garage that a windstorm blew down. Angel went out to ask a few questions, and before Phil could respond, Midas yelled, "Just open your dress." Phil once more stutters and states he has no response to that. Neither do we, and Angel doesn't wear dresses either. Once more, the thought was, "What the hell goes on when I am not home?"

Storm

October 15, 2017

Midas wants everyone to know he has been ready for thirteen minutes...I don't ask.

Chapter 8

This chapter took me a while to figure out how to include without offending anyone. I decided that asking friends (thank you, Mario) would be the best way of including this story as a chapter in Midas's book. The way society is today, I imagine that someone will still be offended but remember, when yelling at friends down the street, you don't know who will hear you. If you don't want anyone using the N-word, don't use it yourself because the person hearing you address your friends in such a manner may not understand the meaning behind you doing so, and this includes little ones of the human race.

Midas doesn't know that it's a racial slur, and neither would any five- or six-year-old child, regardless of skin color. I can't even tell the difference in the way it is being said, and I am told there is a difference. I have been told that between two friends with the word being said with a different accent, it is acceptable.

The problem was, we were friends, just not good friends to where I don't even know if he knew that Midas existed. Personally, I believe the word itself is offensive regardless of how it's said and who it is said to. I will admit, the N-word makes me cringe not only because some of my best friends are African American but because of the negative energy attached to the word itself.

My neighbors on both sides of me are African American and seemed to have large and maybe extended families. The house on the right, though, is the guilty party this time. The mom, who I believed was the head of the household, drove a school bus (which is why Midas does the beeping as if he is backing up that bus himself), and she had a few adult kids living with her. One was her son with his girlfriend and child coming over here and there. The other was a younger man, but not sure where in the family dynamics he fit. I loved them as neighbors except during the summer when the weekend contained a Monday holiday. They would start barbecuing on Friday and continue through Monday's holiday, usually ending their shindig around four Tuesday morning. The whole neighborhood, though, smelled delicious. Dang, her son could *bar-be-cue*, but I am digressing.

My problem with them as neighbors was the older son's friends. Halfway down the block, they would yell the N-word in greeting to each other, with each trying to outdo the other's use of the word, or so it seemed to me. I work Monday through Friday, so I don't know if this was an everyday thing or if his friends were just over on the weekends when I was home.

Just guess which word Midas is now yelling as if he is on the neighbor's best-bud list coming down the block to visit, EXCEPT he is not using the same pronunciation as the two guys used. He sounds like a guy with problems with the neighborhood, using the N-word as if he had issues with some poor soul.

I do know to break a parrot from repeating words; you don't acknowledge them saying it. It is very difficult for one to ignore a parrot screaming certain words over and over, especially when you can hear him outside with all the doors and windows closed. Yes, he was that loud when he screamed it because they would be shouting the word all the way down the block continuously until they reached the door.

If you would have asked me, I would have sworn the blasted bird would get me killed by screaming it on a daily basis. Lucky for him, maybe the neighbors thought it was a lover's quarrel or kids acting like big shots. Although he still says the N-word from time to time, it is safe to say, for the most part, he is over saying it. It also helped with the neighbors moving as there is no one to my knowledge using the word in his hearing range at this time.

I just hope that Midas doesn't get me killed while he is shouting the N-word in the hood because someone addressed his bud half a block away using it as Midas has no filter.

Angel Is Feeling Amused with Storm

June 14, 2019

The moment "fuck a duck" comes outta the mouth, and Midas says, "Quack."

Chapter 9

I love my animals and seldom leave home for any length of time. In 2018, my family wanted to have a family reunion with all my siblings, along with their kids, because my mother was diagnosed with dementia, a.k.a. Alzheimer's and going downhill fast. By the time the family reunion took place, my mother didn't know any of her kids, but Pop (it's what I call my father) was happy to have almost all of his kids home, which was the first time in over twenty years.

Angel and I planned with a friend who did animal boarding and who at that time was willing to accept all my animals, dogs, cats, and birds, into her facility with us providing crates and cages for every one of them, which we had. We were also providing all their food and snacks, plus a little extra for the rescues that they helped with. When it came time to finalize the arrangements and sign the agreement, we found that she sold her portion of the business to her partners.

Talking with people we didn't know about what we discussed with our friend, did not leave us feeling good about leaving our fur babies and feathered friends at this facility anymore. Part of the reason for our uneasiness was because of changed policies, such as they no longer boarded cats. Because we already discussed this prior to signing with our friend, they would agree to board our cats at a slightly higher price and lots of stipulations. Regardless of everything in the paperwork, they absolutely refused to watch our birds, which we had three at the time (a budgie, a lovebird, and, of course, Midas). One gal had a fear of birds, which I understand, and the other thought they were disgusting and dirty and didn't want anything to do with them.

We were down to just a few weeks before the family reunion but because they didn't want to include the birds and the uneasy feeling we had, we decided it wouldn't work any longer, leaving our critters at this facility and started thinking of our other options.

Normally, I would visit my parents, and my daughter would watch the animals. Then the kids would visit, and I would watch the animals. Splitting the number of people showing up at an older household lessens the anxiety of residents living in the house. As much as I love my parents, it was easier for them for us to divide up the number of people visiting, and I usually have a few pups with me, so I don't travel by myself.

Now we had to decide what to do, and I didn't want to be hauling our critters all over the countryside to various people to take care of just for a week or two. Okay, I will admit that I would be worried about not being able to get them back because they fell in love with my cat, dog, or bird. Another scenario would be that the critter pissed them off, and they "gave them away."

Angel and I started asking each other who we knew that could house-sit and not mind taking care of our animals that we could trust. Many of our friends are married with kids, and we know that would not work as they would be divided unless one or the other didn't mind being separated for a few days and nights.

My daughter asked if I would mind if Becky could if Becky is willing. I knew Becky and liked her and said if she would, I don't mind, but for the most part, would she mind the neighborhood, as it would be the deciding factor.

Becky did agree to house and animal sit for us, and needless to say, if you mention Midas to this day, "Fuckin' Midas" comes out of her mouth real quick. She still gets a wee bit irate due to the trauma she endured while housesitting. She did mention that she would never watch our critters again, but I am hoping to convince her to watch the critters once more next summer. Say a prayer that she will.

Did I mention that no one but me can put food in Midas's cage or even clean it? Somedays, even I have problems, and so far, I have been a wee bit faster than Midas. When you are used to Midas, you tend to ignore or get used to what he does because you are around his antics.

Becky would be great at house and animal sitting as a side job; I would even recommend her. She listened to my instructions and even cooked for my critters as I requested. The critters I thought would be a problem were not, and the ones I thought would be angels were not.

Midas was your classic pita (pain in the ass). Of course, he had to be a jerk, and he was proud of himself. He even talked back to Becky, which was unusual, but I am glad she can verify that we don't make up what he says.

I know somewhat what Becky went through, although Midas has only banged his tray at night for Becky. Normally, he bangs the tray on top of his cage during the day, but while I was gone, Midas routinely banged his tray every morning at three.

This is a tone that is very loud and would wake the dead, and he did not stop banging his tray until she came downstairs and yelled at him. She tried doing it from bed, nope; he would do it louder. She tried from the top of the stairs, nope, still didn't stop. She had to literally come down the stairs to tell him to stop, and then he'd laugh at her, all proud of himself.

Another thing he would do was beep the microwave after she left the kitchen and went upstairs. Sometimes, being tired at night, she wouldn't think much of it and go back down to "shut it off" only to find it was never on. And, of course, Midas would laugh at her expense, once again proud of himself. I just hope down the road, Becky can laugh about his antics while she house sat as I know we laugh about it now.

Becky also has her tales now to tell with first-hand experience dealing with Midas for about ten days, which includes some profanity on his part to her, and she heard him loud and clear. You want to get her going on him and hear some of his antics, just ask her about the bird, you'll get a "fucking bird" or "fucking Midas" response, followed by something he did to her, and while she can kind of laugh about most of it now, she still shakes her head at that "fucking bird."

Storm

October 10, 2017

Angel is prepping a dish for work tomorrow, and Midas is yelling, "Is it ready?"

Chapter 10

There are many stories we can tell regarding Midas. Each day brings new conversations and usually new jaw-dropping comments that he has made. Like this morning, he was trying to get Shadow to meow; who knows why. When Shadow didn't meow on his command, he said, "Fuck you."

In 2019, I was going downstairs, which had a gate across the steps to keep the dogs upstairs. As I was getting ready to step over the gate, I realized Anthony, my seven-pound Velcro pup who was eleven years old at the time, was at my feet. As I was trying not to kick him, I lost my balance and fell the rest of the way down the stairs and did a header into the landing, missing the glass window by mere millimeters, barely avoiding going through the landing window. After I cleared the cobwebs from my head (yes, my right shoulder hit the window-pane, and my head hit the wall), I called for my daughter for assistance. She asked if I was okay, and before I could respond, in my voice

Midas said, "Of course." Needless to say, she went back to what she was doing and never came to assist me.

I hobbled upstairs and told her I needed to go to ER, and she stated, "Thought you said you were okay." Once more, before I could answer, Midas yelled, "I am!"

She said, "Oh, shit," grabbed her purse and car keys, and we left for the next four or five hours. I still have issues, but hopefully, everything will be corrected when I take some time to do something about it.

Last night, and by night, I mean we just put all the animals to bed around nine thirty quarter to ten when I saw a few flashlights running outside down my driveway going over through the neighbor's yard, mixing with the flashing lights and sirens that I saw from the landing of my stairs. I guess there was a stolen car a few suburbs away, and I don't know all the details, but, for whatever reason, the thief came down my one-way street the wrong way. Stopped a house or two down from mine with about half dozen police and state trooper cars on each side of the stolen car, blocking the car from leaving (but also blocking me from leaving my own yard).

The police car lights were flashing, lighting up the front yards on both sides of the street in reds and blues for a whole two-plus hours while they were doing whatever investigating they needed to do, which included a tow truck for the stolen car. The sirens were on OUTSIDE of my house for a good thirty to forty-five minutes. Do you know what happens when parrots can hear sounds for any length of time? You got it; we hear loud sirens now, not just the ones he does from a distance but the very loud ones just like they were still outside my door. Good thing I love Midas, and I will ignore him when he does the loud siren in hopes that it will be a short-lived sound that is not needed inside a house.

Midas will talk tomatoes, which he asks on a regular basis. This came about the first summer that we had Midas. I would tell the dogs, "Let's go check the tomatoes" when we were going outside. Guess talking about tomatoes was a way Midas could feel like he was helping with the tomatoes.

Midas also clucks like a chicken and then says, "I'm not a chicken." We now tell him that he looks like a chicken, sounds like a chicken, and probably tastes like a chicken, which makes him a chicken. His responses afterward vary each time from woo-hoos to, oh, fuck. You never know what he will say, which is not good if you are doing a professional video with him in the background.

There were many instances when either Angel or I thought the other responded to the asked question just to find out that Midas was the one who responded. We would have a laugh over the fact that we should know better and that he got us once more.

Another bad habit of Midas is that he likes to talk over me. If I am trying to get Angel's attention when she is upstairs, and I am down or vice versa, he will try to talk over me. It is frustrating for both of us because the other is expecting an answer. I always ask if all the dogs are in bed before I lock the door. He is yelling over me, asking something else, or just trying to outdo me, so Angel doesn't hear me, and I have to ask several times.

Midas will yell, "It's ready, come get it," when Angel is cooking supper. I usually go downstairs to find out it's not ready, but Midas just wants to be included, I am guessing. I don't know why he does it, and yes, he does get away with it because not much can be done to change this behavior.

One fall day, Angel and I were sitting on the front porch just chatting about work and such when it started to get a little chilly. I got up to shut the front door so that Midas wouldn't get chilly. As soon as the front door closed, Midas yelled, "I can't hear you anymore!"

Angel and I started laughing and told Midas to stop his eavesdropping and to get over it. We continued talking on the front porch while listening to him complain about not hearing us anymore and "it's not fair."

In 2011, I was asked to do a presentation on parrots for the AARP. I am not sure how well I did because when I get nervous, I tend to stutter, which leads to some anxiety. It's why I try to stay out of the bigger picture.

I was also asked if I could bring a few birds. Well, of course, I can. I had Midas the second, and yes, I told them he probably would not speak, and he didn't the whole time we were there, but at least they would know what an African gray parrot would look like.

What was most memorable about the presentation wasn't the presentation itself but the trip there. Angel was driving, so I could keep an eye on the birds to make sure they were doing okay.

Midas kept asking Angel if she was lost. It seemed like every five minutes, he would say, "Why aren't we there, are you lost?"

Of course, Angel would argue back that she knew what she was doing, and she wasn't lost, not that she would tell him otherwise even if she was.

Yes, we laugh about it today, but at the time, it was irritating as all heck. Nothing like being put in your place by a bird, especially a bird living in the hood.

Storm

July 19, 2021

Midas's Laugh Corner

Midas yelling: You wanna help
me in the back seat!

Chapter 11

Midas is an old man; exactly how old? We are not sure. He has now been in our house for fourteen, almost fifteen years, and all they knew is that the person who had him before had him for a very long time. Right now, we estimate him to be over forty years old, but for all we know, he could be a lot older as no one knows how long African gray parrots live in captivity. Many fell victim to night frights or other animals in the household before they passed of old age. I mention this once more because I know that when one's number is up, there is nothing anyone can do to prevent it, slow it down a wee bit, but it is going to happen one day, hoping later rather than sooner.

I do know that when Midas passes, the house will be very quiet. He will be missed by many as he has a small fan base because of sharing some of our conversations with our friends, and a few of them got to experience his unique intelligence and witty humor in person. His proverbs, such as "spiders go boing," and many conversations that bring laughter to many will be a gray cloud for a while. So here's to a long life Midas, as I, at this time, can't imagine a quiet house with no Midas bird. Maybe, just maybe, Midas is part cat and has nine lives making me wonder how many lives he has used up. Hopefully, not all of them.

I took a good look at Midas earlier today and thought once more he looked rough around the edges. Maybe he is only here on earth until I finish this book because he is my inspiration. I do hope he is here longer than it takes to publish a book, but I have had fourteen years with him bringing laughter into a world trying to get back on its feet, and that is what is important.

He is part of the reason I get up in the morning; it is to prepare his breakfast and make sure he has bird food and fresh water. Everything that he says or does still brings a smile to my face because even at times, I wonder what the fuck and where in the world did he hear that.

What is truly amazing is how many times we would be talking about one thing or another, and his response is on spot with the conversation. His comments would sound like they were coming from another person and not a bird. Yes, some days, he is on his "stop saying I'm fat" kick or "let's talk tomatoes," but that is Midas trying to get attention and start a conversation. And we will never hesitate to respond to him.

He goes through the you-don't-care-to-stop-calling-me-fat; I do believe are the pre-teenagers running around outside. But one must admit that his wit and conversation are entertaining and, hopefully, will give us many more years of laughter even though we are not sure how to respond.

Tonight, Midas is on a "you just don't care" kick, can't say he's wrong, lol.

**

Angel

December 22, 2010

Would Maddy and Joey please report to Midas—he's been calling you for the last few hours to "come here now" I think you are in BIG trouble That is all.

Angel

September 27, 2011

Oh boy…the joys of having a parrot in the house.

Storm: Midas, what does the kitty say?
Midas: bok bok bok.
Storm: No, she's not the cadbury bunny, Midas, what does the kitty say?
Midas: She's peanut butter and whoo!

~shakes head~ I do not wanna know!

Storm

October 28, 2011

Midas: Joey...JOEY

~~no response~~

Midas: WHERE'S THE BEER?

~~no response~~

Midas: Whadda ya mean it's all gone?

How am I suppose to respond to this...lmao. I don't buy beer that often...and when I do it's for washing my hair or for the tomatoes...I do believe the parrot lost it.

Angel

December 9, 2011

Midas's Laugh Corner

Midas: Whoo whoo. Beat that.
Angel: Whoo whoo, Midas says beat that ha-ha.
Midas: You're not funny!
Angel: I think I'm quite funny.
Midas: You're not being faaaaaaair. Oh shit, you fucker

Storm

February 16, 2012

In the background is Toby Keith's
song "How Do You Like Me Now?!"

Midas: How do you like me now?
Storm: I like you just fine now...
Midas: Then get over here, and
    let me out...
Storm: I am not letting you out...
Midas: Now...
Storm: No...
Midas: Awwwwwwwwwwwwww-
    wwwwwwwwwww.

Storm

March 29, 2012

Those with little ones remember these times (mine now are with an African gray).
I turn on the shower...get in...

Midas: Mom!
Storm: What Midas?
Midas: Mom!
Storm: Midas, I am in the shower... what do you want?
Midas: Nothing.

~~bounces head against shower stall, thinking...I did my time for the crime; my kids are adults...lol~~

Angel

June 3, 2012

So earlier, when Storm was mop-ping the floor,

Midas yells out, "It's wet!"

Ya think? So Storm replies, "Yes, Midas, I know it's wet."

Midas, "Whoo!"

And tonight, we're putting supper away, and he's yelling at us that he's late...sure bird, sure. Lol.

Storm

July 8, 2012

Midas: Mom, come talk to me NOW.
Storm: I am busy, I can't.
Midas: Really?

~~Midas doing sirens~~

Midas: Come talk to me now...
Storm: I'm busy.
Midas: Oh...woooo woooo woooo.

Storm

August 6, 2012

For Sale CUCKOO clock...

Midas: Mom.
Storm: What, Midas?
Midas: You know it's ten o'clock.
Storm: ~~looks at clock~~ No it's
    not...it's only 8:45.
Midas: Mom.
Storm: What, Midas...
Midas:...It's ten o'clock.
~~thought for the day: DAMN
    CUCKOO IS LOCO~~

Angel

August 30, 2012

Angel: Midas, I can still hear you, go to sleep.

Midas: ~mumbles~

Angel: Good night!

Midas: Smart-ass.

Angel (to Storm): Did he just call me a smart-ass?

Storm: I think so.

Midas: Starts to whistle

Angel: Uh-huh, thought so. And then he whistles.

Midas: Do I care?

Angel: I should hope not, but good night!

It's now all quiet, but for how long? Tune in tomorrow for another episode of Midas, the smart-mouthed bird.

Storm

September 2, 2012

Midas's Corner, and I am not laughing...

Midas...Mom.

~~silence~~

Midas...Mom.
Storm...She died.
Midas...That's not funny now...
Angel Roze...I think he said that's
    not funny now...
Storm...That's what I heard...
Midas...Mom...
Storm...Grrrrrrrrrrrrrrrrrrrrrrrrrrrrrrrrrrrrrrrrrrrrrrrrrr

Angel

September 3, 2012

Midas's Corner

Midas: Hey! I want your blood.
Angel: You can't have it! Vampire!
Midas: What!
Angel: You heard me! Vampire!
Midas: Mom!
Storm: What, Midas.
Midas: I gotta fry this now!
Angel: Midas, you're a freak!
Midas: What?
Angel: You heard me!
Midas: Whoo!
We ain't asking!

Angel

September 3, 2012

Midas's Laugh Corner

Midas: Mᴏᴏᴍ!
Storm: Midas!
Midas: It's six o'clock now!
Storm: It's not six o'clock now.
Midas: Mᴏᴍ!
Storm: Midas!
Midas: It's six o'clock now.
Storm: It's not six o'clock now.
Midas: Mᴏᴍ!
Storm: Midas!
Midas: It's six o'clock now.
Storm: It's not six o'clock now.
Midas: Shut the fuck up!
Storm: Midas! You're gonna get soap in your beak!

I start laughing, and Midas starts laughing and cackling, lol.

Storm

September 28, 2012

Midas's Laugh Corner...

~~whistles...sirens~~

Midas...Mom.
Storm...What, Midas?
Midas...I'm fucking drunk now...
Angel...Did he say I'm fucking
    drunk NOW?
Storm...Sounded like it...
Midas...I'm fucking drunk.

    Maybe I was hearing things?
Although I know it's a favorite line
of the neighbors~~SOAP

Storm

September 29, 2012

Midas's Laugh Corner...

Midas...MOM.
Storm...Midas.
Midas...What do you want?
Storm...WHAT DO YOU WANT?
Midas...Mom, we need to talk now...
Storm...Go ahead and talk now...
Midas...I don't wanna.
Boy, do I feel a headache coming on!

Angel

October 27, 2012

The things I've learned from Midas
in the past one and a half hours…
Midas is God.

Angel: Who do you think you are?
Midas: God.
Me and Storm look at each other
 and crack up. Midas talks to
 the animals we've had that
 he's never known.
Midas: Dakotah, are you upstairs?
Dakotah was my pom mix from
 four years ago…say wha? If
 he's upstairs, we got problems!
Midas still wants to get drunk.
Midas: Mooom.
Storm: What, Midas?
Midas: I wanna talk NOW!
Storm: So talk.
Midas: Mooooom.
Storm: What, Midas?
Midas: Come here, I wanna get
 drunk now!
Storm: Well, you go get drunk
 then.

Midas: Moom, I'll bring you a soda.

Storm looks at me, "How is it that he can go get drunk, and I get a soda?"
Least he has a designated driver?

Angel

December 11, 2012

Midas's Laugh Corner...

Midas is talking and making noises.

Angel: Midas, good night!
Midas: Can I think about it?
Angel: No! You can't think about it, good night!
Midas: Oooohhh...

All this while I'm talking to Storm about Apollo's new antics. He tips the food dish to spill some out in front of him so he can lay down and eat in front of one of the food dishes. Now apparently, he's spilling some into piles in front of the other dogs around him. Guess at least he feeds others too. Oh boy.

Storm

December 16, 2012

Midas's Laugh Corner...

The art of ignoring a bird...not easy...

Midas...Mom...IT'S NOT FAIR.
~~silence~~
Midas...Mom...IT'S NOT FAIR.
~~silence~~
Midas...Mom...DO YOU HEAR ME?
ME...YES, I hear you...get over it.
Midas...I just want to tell you it's
    not fair...
ME...~~grumble, grumble~~
Midas...BUT IT'S NOT FAIR
Will someone PLEASE break the
    record...
~~grumble, grumble~~

Storm

April 13, 2013

Midas's Laugh Corner

This is Midas's statement of the day...

Midas...I am completely pissed off.

Hmmm, wonder who peed in his Wheaties this morning.

Storm

May 15, 2013

Midas's Laugh Corner...

Angel Roze to her pup...Give me a kiss.

Angel Rose...You don't love me anymore?

Midas...Booooooo HOOOOOOOOOOOOOOO!

Okay...I can stop laughing now...lol.

Storm

June 4, 2013

Midas's Laugh Corner

Midas...Mom, I wanna talk now.

Storm...Talk, and I will pretend to listen

Midas...I'm pissed off...

What does a parrot have to be pissed off at? Wait, maybe he is pissed at me...lmao.

Storm

September 18, 2013

Midas's Laugh Corner
(a.k.a. Kitty Terrorist)

Scenario—Midas leaving his cage and wandering over to the kitty kennel to try to attack Shadow (who even at five months is quite large, and Spitfire, who is not that much behind her brother).

Storm...MIDAS BACK TO YOUR BED
Midas...No.
Me grabbing water bottle and spraying Midas
Midas attacking the water bottle...
Midas...You give up
Storm...No I don't give up, get back to your bed.
Midas...You bad.
Storm...No...you are bad... back to your bed if you want breakfast...
Midas...No

Needless to say...Midas is back in his bed with his breakfast...I WON only because I am bigger...yay me!

Storm

November 12, 2013

Midas's Laugh Corner

Midas...Mom.
Storm...What, Midas?
Midas...Mom, come here
Storm...Midas, I am right here...
    what do you want?
Midas...You are still there...
Storm...Midas, I am right here...
Why...OH, WHY don't I stuff him for
    Thanksgiving dinner...Have a
    great day everyone

Storm

December 5, 2013

Midas's Laugh Corner...

Asked Angel Roze if Beverly could be her social secretary, and Angel yelled back...I dont have any social life to have one, and Midas yelled, "WANNA GO OUT WITH ME?" I am here laughing my fat butt off...lmao.

Angel

December 15, 2013

It's bad enough when you got smart dogs...even worse when you got smart cats...damn cats... and the bird doesn't help either!

Last night, I was heating soup up for Storm, and the damn cat (namely Shadow) jumped up on the sink next to the stove, which was ON. I yelled at him, and he just looks at me like, "What?" So I spanked him, and again he looks at me like, "What?"...sticks his nose up in the air, jumps down and STRUTS out of the kitchen. I'm mumbling about damn cats near the stove, if the burner would have been higher, he would have hit the flame and caught on fire...I yelled at him, "What are you trying to do, burn yourself?" and Midas (God love him) yells back loudly..."YEAH," and then cackles...~shakes head~ Thanks, Midas, don't need your help. Seriously...the cat meows in the morning if we're not down-stairs at 6 a.m...and if the dogs start early, so does the cats! AND they'll meow when we get home if we're not fast enough getting the dogs out and letting them out. I'd like to think just ONCE I RUN the house, not the animals...

But we all know I'd be lying to myself then too, as the animals run the house, not the humans... just ONCE, I'd want a stupid ani-mal, but then again, I'd prolly have a hard time with that too... lol ~shakes head~

Storm

December 21, 2013

Midas's Laugh Corner...

Midas...MOM, COME HERE.
Midas...Mom, what's your name?
Storm: You already know my
    name...it's MOM.
Midas: Stop being a smart-ass.

Dear Santa, along with everything else I need, would you
please bring Midas some man-
ners? Grrrrrrrrrrrrrrrrrrrrrrrrrrrrrrrrrrrrrrr.

Storm

December 29, 2013

Midas's Laugh Corner...

Midas...MOM, we have to talk
    now.
Storm...Go to sleep, it's bedtime.
Midas...You are just trying to piss
    me off.
Storm...Go to sleep...
Midas...but Mom we have to talk
    now.

I think I need to have my house sound proof so Midas cannot hear what the neighbors say when fighting...and does he really get pissed off...he is a parrot hmmm will find out when I feed him in the morning...grrrrrrrrrrrrrrrrrrrrrrrrrrrr.

Angel

December 31, 2013

Midas's Laugh Corner

Midas: Sit. Sit. Good Girl. ~makes
    explosive sounds~
Angel: Midas, you can't blow up
    the dogs like that!
Midas: Sit. Stay. ~explosive sound~
Angel: Midas, that's not right!
Midas: Whoo!

~shakes head~ Good grief.

Storm

January 29, 2014

Midas's Laugh Corner...

~The usual dogs/cats/parrot noise followed by...

Midas: Hey, jerk face.
Storm...What do you mean jerk face?
Midas: Yes, you are...
Storm...You better watch it...
Back to normal...sort of.
Midas: I live here.
Angel Roze: That can be changed.
Midas: No, it cant.

It's way too early for this conversation...if it wasn't for work... ~shakes head~

Storm

February 21, 2014

Midas's Laugh Corner...or Not

I believe Midas is just a smart-ass...
scenario this morning...

~pup spits up, and I go to wipe
up the mess...while bent over (in
my night shirt), Shadow jumps
underneath as I stand up, as he
likes to "hide and scare" pups...

Me to Shadow...What do you
think you are doing?

Midas...He's just helping...

Me...He is not helping...

Midas...Fuck you.

WHY ME...WHY, OH, WHY ME...I love
my critters...

Angel

April 13, 2014

Midas's Laugh Corner

Midas: Mooom, we need to talk now!

Storm: We'll talk tomorrow.

Midas: Well, I want you to knock it off!

Storm: When you can pay my bills, then I'll knock it off.

Midas: ~singsong voice~
Ooooookkkkkaaaaaayyyyy.

I busted out laughing, and then he yells, "Don't poop in here!"
~falls over laughing~

Angel

September 10, 2014

Midas's Laugh Corner

Abigayle barks upstairs, Shadow is in the kitchen playing under the cupboard and runs upstairs after she barks, and Midas yells, "Go beat 'em up!"

Followed a little later by,

Midas: What are you doing here!
Storm: I live here, what's your
    excuse?
Midas: Well, that's not fair!

Angel

October 29, 2014

Midas's Laugh Corner

So apparently I pushed Midas down when I went downstairs, he said so...

Midas: Don't push me down!
Storm: Angel, don't push Midas down!
Angel: Awwww, you ruin all my fun. Midas, you're a tattletale.
Midas: You pissed me off.

So apparently not only did I push him down, I pissed him off. I blamed Belle. Lol.

Angel Is with Storm

November 2, 2014

Midas Proverbs:

"You gotta go meow to fuck things up"
　　Glad we're clear on that!

Angel Is with Storm.

November 5, 2014

Midas Proverbs:

"Spiders go BOING!"

Storm

December 27, 2014

Midas's Laugh Corner...

Midas: I'm talking.
Midas: Meooooow.
Storm: Really?

Angel Is with Storm

January 13, 2015

Midas's Laugh Corner...

He's talking up a storm down-stairs, and he just cracked me up!

Midas: I'm a bad puppy. Woo-hoo!

~raises eyebrow~ Really?
Followed by some puppy barking and a "what are you doing here" puppy bark, puppy bark...

Storm

March 3, 2015

Midas's Laugh Corner...

We all know the neighborhood is crap that I live in, and I know that we hear repeats of what is yelled down the street. Thank you, Midas, for the laugh tonight.

Midas...We all know its crap...
Me and Angel Roze chuckle.
Midas...WHERE ARE MY FRIENDS NOW.

Angel and I burst out laughing...

Angel

March 10, 2015

Midas's Laugh Corner...

Sooo fire truck is on the street, lights on and what not...dogs are all put to bed downstairs, and Midas (bless him) started scream-ing like girl.

Angel: Oh my god...Midas, NO!

I go to the landing, as usually he won't speak if he sees some-one, and the dogs will stay quiet. Storm goes downstairs.

Storm: Midas, you don't scream when the fire truck is here.
Midas: So shoot people (makes shooting sounds).
Angel: Midas, shhhh!
Midas: ~quietly shooting sounds~

Omg...one of these days...

Storm

May 15, 2015

Midas's Laugh Corner...

Midas: Someone let me out.
Me...I ain't going to let you out.
Midas:...Crap, I knew that...

What a conversation first thing
in the morning...~~laughing~~

Storm

May 26, 2015

Midas's Laugh Corner

Me talking to a pup: You are
    going outside.
Midas: Let's get with it.
Angel Roze: I don't have to get
    with it.
Midas: Well, are you with it?

Some of the conversations in
my house...

Storm

June 13, 2015

Midas's Laugh Corner...

Saturday night...Angel made popcorn and poured milk for us... yells, "Mom, I need help."

Midas yells...She's waiting.
Storm...I know, I am on my way.
Midas...It's a miracle.
Storm...Not really...
Midas...I have a bat...

Hmmmm...wonder what kind of bat he has...

Storm

July 23, 2015

Midas's Laugh Corner...

Okay...it is funny, but maybe not to him...because he is screaming that he cannot have friends over because I won't let him out...
That is my parrot for you...

Midas's Laugh Corner...

Angel...Go to sleep.
Midas...making odd noises
Dogs start to bark/howl (mostly due to fireworks).
Angel...Quiet.
Midas...You can't make them do that.
dogs continue to bark/howl
I clap my hands to get their attention.
dogs get quiet
Midas yells: You made it deaf in here...
Still laughing...got to love the conversations with Midas T Byrd.

Angel Is with Storm

July 29, 2015

Midas's Laugh Corner

Midas: whimpers and cries like a
    puppy
Angel: Midas, you are not a
    puppy, stop it.
Midas: It's Isabella.
Angel: No, it's not, she's outside
    with Mom.
Midas: Awwww, but I live here.
Angel: You may live here, but
    you're not a puppy.
Midas: I'll kick your ass.
Angel: Go ahead, you're still not
    a puppy.
Midas: That's enough! ~whimpers
    and cries again~ It's Isabella.

I'm laughing so hard I can't
respond right now, lol.

Angel Is with Storm.

August 6, 2015

Midas's catch phrases of late?

"It sucks to be you!" and "I want to see you!"
Gee, thanks bird!

Angel Is with Storm.

August 6, 2015

So tonight while cooking dinner, Midas accused me of poisoning him. Then he told me to stop following him. And to top it off, he asked if he could spin my head. I don't think so!

Storm

August 7, 2015

As a heads up...last year, Midas started "singing" ♫♪♫ Frosty the snowman ♫♪♫ in August, which he never did before, he waited until he heard it on the radio at Christmas time...guess what he is trying to sing now...♫♪♫ Frosty the Snowman ♫♪♫...let's hope that the winter does not start early, and the snow is not enough to support snowman life...hopefully Midas, as a weatherman, is as wrong as often as they are...

We laughed for a good five minutes, lol.

Angel

August 11, 2015

Oh my god...still lmao

Midas's Laugh Corner

Don't remember what smart-ass remark he made, but the following conversation couldn't have gotten any better:

Storm: You're not my mama or
    my papa so.
Midas: Snap to it, boy!

    I laughed.

Storm: Midas, one, I'm not a boy,
    and the only snapping around
    here is gonna be your neck if
    you keep it up
Midas: Aw, fuck it.

    I laughed harder.
    Midas mumbled a bit and said something with shit in it, lol.

I really gotta get all this on tape sometime. He never does the good stuff when I record, lol.

Storm

October 10, 2015

Midas's Laugh Corner...

Dogs are barking (had FedEx here)

Storm: Quiet...
Midas: In a minute.
Storm: It's right now, not in a minute.
Midas: Quiet.
Midas: Lay down.

Tell me where did I lose control of ruling over my own house... King Midas, where is my gold? Oh, it's in our conversations, but I am not telling him that.

Midas takes the cake tonight... he is cutting down everyone tonight...

Storm

October 27, 2015

Midas's Laugh Corner...

I am cooking supper, Angel is talking to me...Midas is being Midas...

Angel is correcting the dogs for picking on Spitfire...

Midas...Stop saying that.

Angel...I can say whatever the hell I want.

Midas...Stop talking that way

I start laughing, Angel flips off Midas, and Midas starts on the tirade of "sucks to be you."

Storm

November 6, 2015

Midas's Laugh Corner

Midas...MOM, WE GOT TO TALK.
Storm...We will talk tomorrow.
Midas...Well, it sucks to be you.
Storm...Only sucks to be me
    because I have you.
Midas...You can't say that.

~hits head~...Why me, Lord?
Got to love Midas.

Angel

November 12, 2015

Midas's Laugh Corner

Storm and I were talking in the hallway, Midas was talking to himself...and then it went like this:

Storm: (Picks up kitty, and she starts to purr loudly.)
Angel: There she goes, purring away.
Storm: All you gotta do is touch her.
Midas: Just like most girls.
Angel: That was highly inappropriate Midas!
Midas: (Silence.)

Few mins later, he yelled something about wanting his hair done.
~blinks~ Riiiiight!

Angel

January 1, 2016

Midas's Laugh Corner...

Midas: Mom, we need to talk now.

Angel: It can wait forever.

Storm: ~sings~ And ever, and ever, and ever.

Midas: Fine, I'm to pissed off to talk now.

~laughs~ We're both rolling... oh, Midas, how you entertain at times!

Storm

March 6, 2016

Midas's Laugh Corner...

Midas's quote for today...
    Midas...Mom, we need to talk tomato, dumbass.
    Grrrrr...what to do, what to do.

.

Storm

April 3, 2016

Midas's Laugh Corner...

Okay, it's me laughing, as Midas
just yelled at Angel
...."You're a pain in my ass."

Storm

May 8, 2016

Midas's Laugh Corner...

Midas: You are way too fat.
Angel: What do you know.
Midas: I don't owe you.

~still chuckling~...and sometimes it just flows out of his mouth...

Angel Is with Storm

July 1, 2016

Midas's Laugh Corner…

I'm upstairs taking care of the dog kennels, and Midas is downstairs doing his usual noises and ramblings…then I hear:

Midas: I'll kick your ass, you're guilty!

~insert Midas doing a police siren~
Oy vey!

Angel Is with Storm

July 31, 2016

Yup, so Storm is outside with the dogs, and Midas is just carrying on while I take care of water and a few other things before the pups come in...and what is he yelling today?

Midas: I'm gonna kick your ass.
Angel: I'd like to see you try!
Midas: Get your ass down here. (Whistles.)
Angel: Not gonna happen, boy, but nice try!
Midas: Whoop! Gonna kick your ass. (Whistles twice.)

I'm laughing, and anyone who knows us knows we can't whistle worth a hoot. I'm usually telling the dogs to go downstairs and outside, or to their beds, never get down here, lmao...makes me really wonder what's been going on in the neighborhood!

Storm

December 4, 2016

Midas's Laugh Corner

How do you respond when he is
yelling..."You wanna do me?"

Storm

December 31, 2016

Midas is meowing like a cat
in heat...~~shaking head~~

Angel was with Storm

January 14, 2017

Midas's Laugh Corner...

Storm and I were in the kitchen while she was cooking supper and well...Midas...need I say anything more:

Midas yells: I'm on my period! (I might point out we never say that. We have other phrases we use.)
Angel: You want some chocolate?
Midas: I'll kick your ass.

Storm and I were both laughing, of course, and he's mumbling under his breath, and then on the way upstairs he whines:

Midas: I'm faaaaaaaaaaaaat.

~shakes head~ Really, Midas?

Angel

January 21, 2017

~giggles and laughs~

Midas just yelled, "Spank me, I don't care!"
Really, Midas?

Storm

May 14, 2017

Midas's Laugh Corner...

Not sure who he is talking to, but his one-liner for today...

Midas: Not sure, but do you have a brain?

Angel Is with Storm

March 15, 2017

Midas's Laugh Corner

Midas: It's ready!
Storm: No, it's not!
Midas: It's not my problem!
Storm: It can be!
Midas: Its ready!
Storm: No, it's not!
Midas: Well, that makes me upset!
Storm: Not my problem!

Then he breaks out into singing "Frosty."
I told him to shut his mouth!
I'm dying, and I know I missed more of that convo that was good too but typing on the phone and listening doesn't always work.

Storm Is with Angel

May 26, 2017

Midas's Laugh Corner...

As we get breakfast ready for birds and pups...
Midas for the millionth time...
Is it ready?
Storm for the millionth time...
No.
Midas...Dumbass.
Angel breaks out in laughter... got to love him—the dumbass.

Storm Is Feeling Amused

August 1, 2017

Midas's Laugh Corner

Midas: ISABELLA.
Midas: Isabella gonna spank yer ass.
Midas: Isabella, are you okay?

OKAY...Midas...just remember, Isabella is the good pup...and nothing like giving an ass whooping, and then checking to make sure she is okay...I do love my critters, including Midas.

Storm

December 15, 2017

Midas's Laugh Corner

Me yelling at a pup to leave the cats alone...

Midas: GET YOUR HANDS OFF ME!

Me and Angel ~~shakes our head~~

Midas: GET YOUR HANDS UP!

WTF has been going on while I've been at work.

Storm

December 26, 2017

Midas's Laugh Corner...

Something falls in the kitchen, I yell at Angel, "You okay?"

Angel yells back, "I'm okay!"

Midas yells, "Not by a long shot."

I am still trying not to laugh... lmao.

Storm Is with Angel

February 12, 2018

Midas's Laugh Corner

Angel and I was discussing the death of a country artist, and what we believe was the cause— no disrespect to him or his family was intended.

Storm:...Possible heart attack because he was a big guy.
Angel...He was and I don't mean fat...just a big guy.
Midas...JUST SAY HE'S FAT.

I thought I had no tact, but Midas.

Angel

February 22, 2018

I'm prepping beds for the pups,
and Storm is outside with the pups
and Midas…

Midas: Dante! Dante! Good boy!
Me: Midas, Dante is outside.
Midas: Sit, sit!
Me: Midas, everyone is outside.
Midas: Whew!
    Really?

Storm

April 28, 2018

How to quiet Midas...give him popcorn.

Storm Is with Angel

May 3, 2020

Midas just yelled, "Stop saying
'fuck you, Isabella!'"
    Lord, give me strength.

Storm

May 13, 2018

Midas's Laugh Corner

Angel telling me about the kisses she got from the pups—Isabella and Cleopatra for putting them on my bed.

Midas: Can you stomach that...

Me and Angel start laughing... lmao.

Storm

June 2, 2018

Midas told Angel that she needed a permit to kick his ass ~~where to find said permit~~

Storm

June 2, 2018

Midas's Laugh Corner

Dogs are barking

Midas: You bark like a girl.

Angel Is with Storm

December 5, 2019

Midas's Laugh Corner...

Storm and I were in the kitchen, and it goes something like this:

Midas: JERK!
Angel: You're a JERK!
Midas: (singsong voice) F-F-FUCK Yoooou!
Angel: Fuck you too!
Storm: You gotta get the F-F-Fuck Yooou up there.
Midas: I'm peeeeeing!

Really? Since when do we sing it? And I really don't need to know what he's doing, lol.

Storm Is with Angel

July 13, 2020

After getting home from work and walking through the front door and seeing Midas's cage empty.

Angel says, "Okay, Midas, where the fuck are you?"

His cage door was open, and no Midas that you can see. I walk in and see the empty cage and say the same thing...

Storm: Okay, Midas, where the fuck are you?
Midas as he peeks over the back edge of his cage: Woooo-hooooo...
Me and Angel: Boo.

Lmao, as Angel gives him a broom ride and puts him back in his cage...He got another broom ride and caused a wee bit of panic...

Storm Is with Angel

July 13, 2020

Midas is on a roll tonight as he was singing "Frosty the Snowman," and I told him he was murdered—his coal was used to start a fire in which his arms were ripped off to use to roast marshmallows...he was doing his mournful sounding... ohhhhhhhhhhhhhhhhhhhhhhs.

Storm Is with Angel

July 27, 2020

Midas's Laugh Corner

Midas has been making sounds like gunfire—A LOT lately so each time he does, I yell... "I want to livvvvvvvve."

Tonight, its continuous "gunfire."

Midas: Pew, pew, pew.
Storm: I want to live...
Midas: Pew, pew, pew, pew...
I start going upstairs...
Midas: I'm getting rid of idiots... pew pew pew.

Me dying from laughing, and I don't want to know but hoping he is taking care of the bodies; otherwise, Angel will have to deal with them in the morning...
#NotBoringWithMidas

Storm Is with Angel

August 19, 2020

Midas is yelling things like:

Midas: I wanna talk tomato.
Midas: It makes me sad.
Storm: That's enough, Midas, put
    a cork in it...
Midas: I DID, BUT IT WON'T GO.

    Angel almost choked laugh-
ing, but neither of us is asking...

Angel Is with Storm

August 24, 2020

Midas's Laugh Corner

We just put everyone to bed, said good night to Midas as we go upstairs...

I heard him yell something but wasn't paying attention, and then:

Midas: You don't have to ignore me!

Angel: I can ignore you if I want to!

Midas: So do it real quick!

I thought I was to start with questions.

Angel Is with Storm.

November 25, 2020

Midas's Laugh Corner

Had to run upstairs so I could post this one...

Midas: Doing whistles and clapping noises (we clap to get dogs attention). Come here! Come Here! *whistles and claps* Come here!

Mom: Do I look like a dog that's going to come when you call?

Midas: You look like me! *whistles and claps*

Mom and I look at each other and shake our heads. Really?

Angel Is with Storm.

December 7, 2020

Kinda sad when your authority is undermined by the bird. This morning, I was correcting Dante, and telling him he was being a bad boy, and Midas starts yelling, "Dante! Good boy!" Uh, no!

Storm Is with Angel

December 14, 2020

Midas's Laugh Corner...

Midas: How can I help?
Storm: By being good.
Midas: Try again.

Did I get a Magic 8-ball response or what? F——cking bird.

Storm

December 20, 2020

Went to YouTube and pulled up the video of "Frosty the Snowman." Midas watched it twice, making comments here and there. When Frosty was done counting, Midas replied, "Good job."

Storm with Angel

December 23, 2020

Midas's Laugh Corner...

Midas and Angel are having a screaming match...

Midas: COME HERE!
Angel: I'm right here.
Midas: I SAID RIGHT HERE!
Midas: Let me out!
Angel: I'm not letting you out.
Midas: LET ME OUT!
Angel: I'M NOT LETTING YOUR FUCKING ASS OUT!
Midas: LET ME OUT!
Angel: Nobody cares.
Midas: I don't care.
Angel: I don't either.
Midas: You are just saying I'm fat...
Angel: Will you stop yelling?
Midas: YOU DON'T CARE!
MIDAS: HEY, YOU, I'M JUST SAYING!

This has been their conversation for the night...and he is yelling

at the top of his itty-bitty lungs...I
am upstairs laughing...Midas is in
rare form tonight.

Storm Is with Angel

December 23, 2020

Midas's Laugh Corner...

Midas: What do you want?
Storm: For you to be good.
Midas: Too bad.

What is he going to do, go through all the Magic 8-ball answers...I think he suckered me into this this morning...Damn bird.

Storm Is with Angel

December 29, 2020

Midas's Laugh Corner...

Angel and I were talking in the dining room discussing the day:

Midas: Is Christopher here?
Storm: No, Midas, he's not here.
Midas: Did you kill him?
Storm: No, MIDAS, I didn't kill him.
Midas: Is he dead?
Storm: No, he's not dead...
Midas: What you drinking?
Storm: Milk, and it's actually none
    of your business.
Midas: Just go to bed.

WTF—Why me, Lord? Midas was in rare form today. Bossy little...He asked, "Mom, let's talk tomatoes...oh, fuck it," before I could even respond; we will talk tomatoes tomorrow...sheeesh.

Storm

January 2021 (wasn't posted)

Midas. How can I help?
Me. By being good.
Midas. Good luck.

Another Magic 8-ball answer—what the heck is with this? And I haven't responded to his what do you want; how can I help with questions lately?

Storm Is with Angel

January 4, 2021

Midas's Laugh Corner...

Storm coming upstairs, and the dogs start barking...

Storm to the barking dogs: KNOCK IT OFF!

Dogs continue barking.
Storm to the barking dogs: What did I say?

Midas: KNOCK IT OFF!
Midas: Rocket sounds going off...

I asked...but I didn't ask Midas...there was no response needed...and I didn't explode or set off any rockets either...

Storm Is with Angel

January 23, 2021

Midas's Laugh Corner...

Midas: Quiet

Storm:...continues on to the kitchen

Storm: Maybe you should say "talk to me" or "say something please"

Midas: Shuddup

Storm: That's not nice, Midas.

I open the front door and go to lock up, as I am leaving.

Midas: Can I go with?

Me: No, Midas, you can't...you have to stay home...be good.

Sadly, I left and didn't hear what he had to say...but telling Mom to shut up is not a way to get something you want...BAD BIRD.

Angel Is with Storm

Midas's Laugh Corner...

Get home, walk in the door, and...

Midas: Be quiet!
Angel: You can't tell me what to
    do!
Storm: In other words, you're not
    her mother.

I say that's right, and Mom walks by him, and he tells her to "keep moving."

We're so loved when we get home, lol.

Midas Proverb: You can listen with one ear.

Angel Is with Storm

March 16, 2021

I think it's a lil dangerous to go downstairs...we're hearing a lot of "shooting" and "missiles/ fireworks" going off and...some cackling...who's going first?

HAHAHA...Midas just yelled at Mom, "YOU TALKING TO ME?"

Angel Is with Storm.

April 6, 2021

So Mom and I are talking in the kitchen while heating up dinner (it's warm-ups tonight, yay!)... and the following conversation takes place:

Midas (yelling): You calling me a
    bastard!?
Us after looking at each other with
    mouths dropped: Not yet!
Midas: Whatever. I'll kick your
    head in!
We started laughing and then,
Midas: Moooom! Wanna talk
    tomato?
Mom: I wouldn't dare while you're
    kicking heads in!
Midas: It's good for you!

Of course, we're looking at each other and laughing while shaking our heads...since when is getting your head kicked in good for you? Midas is on a roll tonight!

Storm Is with Angel

June 10, 2021

Midas's Laugh Corner

Midas is singing/whistling like one of the birds outside—it's pretty, and I do like the sound

Storm: Midas, are you a songbird?
Midas: No.

Grumbles for a few then…

Midas: Can we talk tomatoes that's fat?

Angel Is with Storm

June 24, 2021

Midas's Laugh Corner...

Doing this just after it happened, lol, as we just got home a few minutes ago and are working on getting dogs and cats all setup and out...dogs are outside with Mom while I'm getting foods/waters ready and such and it goes like this:

Midas: Whistles and clicks.
Shadow (cat): Meow.
Midas: Does the finger snap and
    clap sounds
Shadow: Meow
Midas: Shut up!
Shadow: Meoooow.
Midas: Finger snaps.
Shadow: Meowwww.
Midas: I said be quiet!
Shadow: Meowww.
Midas: Shadow, Come here!
    ~clap sounds~ Come here
    right now!

Shadow: Meow

Midas: Don't you hear me! Come here ~finger snaps~ no one hears me!

Me (shouts downstairs): Midas, I don't think he's going to listen to you!

Midas: Come here ~finger snaps~ Hear me!

I'm dying laughing upstairs. Sorry, I don't snap to anyone, lmao. I so wish I could have gotten that on at least audio!

Storm

July 19, 2021

Midas's Laugh Corner

Midas yelling: You wanna help
me in the back seat!

Storm Is with Angel

July 31, 2021

Midas's Laugh Corner

Upstairs, Angel and I are arguing
about who picked the last game.
 Midas yells...Stop slow dancing up there...

Me: We are not slow dancing.
Midas: Awwwwwwwwwwwww,
 bummer.

Both of us start laughing...

Angel Is with Storm

September 2, 2021

Tonight, Midas is on "you just don't care" kick...can't say he's wrong, lol.

Angel Is with Storm

September 17, 2021

Midas's Laugh Corner

Got the dogs out to bed, and we go upstairs shutting lights off and tell Midas good night...we get upstairs and then...

Midas: I WANNA SEE YOU!
Angel: But I don't want to see you, good night!
Storm: Why do you want to see me, Midas?
Midas: I CAN'T SEE YOU!
Storm: Of course, you can't see me, I'm upstairs, Midas, good night!
Midas: DON'T SAY THAT!
Storm: I already did, good night, Midas, it's bedtime!
Midas: YOU DON'T CARE, I WANNA SEE YOU!

Mumbles some things under his breath that I prolly don't want to know, and Mom and I are dying laughing.

There's your laugh for the day/night or both.

Angel

November 4, 2021

Midas's Laugh Corner

So Mom (Storm) and I were talking upstairs. Midas yells something, I yelled back (don't remember now what it was about as what comes out of his mouth made me forget everything else).

Midas (yelling): Don't have a calf!
I looked at Mom...calf? wtf?
Mom: Calf/Cow about the same.
Angel (yelling): Mooo, Midas, mooo!

Mom and I are laughing as well, technically calf would come before a cow? Lol.

Few hours later, dogs are in bed, we are winding down. and sirens fly by the house. and it's like okay...and then more sirens come by and surround the area and lights (police). Mom sees two people with flashlights run by the

side of the house into the neighbors backyard as she was going
downstairs...and she comes
back up to tell me this...so shit...
lights are in front of the house,
sirens were going on for a bit, I'm
in the bathroom taking my polish
off my nails, and Midas is having
a ball doing sirens downstairs. So
we are yelling at him to hush it,
Mom goes to the crime page to
see if she can spot what is going
on, and he's doing sirens, and
the garbled talk, and Mom said
something about she wonders if
they got 'em in cuffs and

Midas yells: Wooooo! Got 'em!

Man, oh man...it's been wild
tonight, I wish I had a record-
ing of all the stuff he was saying!
Course, we're also trying to hush
him. So glad we put the dogs to
bed when we did, or wow, that'd
have been a mess and a half!
Looks like everything is picked
up / cleaned up, and they are
gone now, so off to bed I go! So
much for going to bed early, lol.

Angel

November 8, 2021

Midas's Laugh Corner

Mom (Storm) and I were chatting in the kitchen, and Midas yells, "Are you done crying yet?" And then it was something about "gettin' over it."

A little while later, we were getting ready to wrap things up in the kitchen since it's bedtime, and Midas asked if I wanted my head exploded. I told him he's an asshole, and that's not kosher... and then, apparently, I got exploded. I'm now headless, and he don't care I guess I'm done cryin'? Lmao.

Storm

November 23, 2021

Tuesday morning getting breakfast ready for the animals, Midas
is making his usual comments,
suddenly yells,

Midas: Don't shoot me!
Storm: I didn't.
Midas: Okay, pew pew pew.

Okay, you can shoot me but
I can't shoot you...what happened in the neighborhood that I
am not aware of because it's not
something we would say...

Storm

November 26, 2021

2021 Midas's Laugh Corner...

Midas: Purring like the cats (Shadow has a very loud purr).
Me: Midas you are not a cat
Midas: Get over it...

If only he was my size...but he is Midas, and I actually wouldn't expect less than a smart butt comment from him...Love you, Midas.

Angel Is with Storm

December 1, 2021

Midas's Laugh Corner

So this morning went like this,

Midas(yelling): What are you doing?

Mom: Getting your breakfast.

Angel: Midas, you want your breakfast right?

Midas (singsongy voice): No, I want a puppy.

Really? I told him he has several and doesn't take care of them. I didn't get an answer back.

Storm Is with Angel

December 20, 2021

I am talking to the dogs...and leave it to Midas.

Storm quieting the dogs from barking.

Midas: Quiet.
Storm: I don't have to be quiet in
    my own house.
Midas: Meeeeeeeeeeooooooooooow!
Angel: You're not a cat
Midas: That's just not fair.
Storm: Get over it.
Midas: You are just calling me fat.

Why can't I get the last word in...

Storm Is with Angel

December 25, 2021

Midas's Laugh Corner...

Midas lets out a loud "girlie type" scream.

Midas: That will get you into
    trouble.
Angel: It will get someone in
    trouble.
Midas: I WANT A PUPPY.
Angel: You ain't getting a puppy.
Midas: Fuck you.

    Now Midas is cackling like the wicked witch of the north... It doesn't stop unless he is being recorded...would be nice if he yelled "MERRY CHRISTMAS, EVERYONE..."

About the Author

Donita Kordonowy was born and raised in Sidney, Montana. Her parents lived in a house that her father built himself, along with her mother, three sisters, and a brother. After a second failed marriage, Donita moved to Rochester, New York, with her two children, three dogs, and fifty parrots.

Donita always loved animals and spent hours trying to save them all. During her second marriage, Donita spent free time rescuing unwanted birds, learning everything she could from other bird breeders, and reading many books. After spending time working with the birds she rescued, she found homes when possible.

Today, Donita works as a secretary, takes care of her animals, crafts using various mediums, and does transports for animal rescues.